Tips for Talking and Reading Together

Stories are a fun and reassuring way of introducing children to new experiences.

- Talk about the title and the pictures on the cover.
- Talk about your child's expectations and emotions.
- Read the story with your child.
- Have fun finding the hidden toothbrushes.

When you've read the story:

- Discuss the Talk About ideas on page 27.
- Look at the tooth brushing instructions on pages 28–29.
- Do the fun activity at the end.

Have fun!

Find the toothbrushes hidden in every picture.

At the Dentist

Roderick Hunt • Annemarie Young

Alex Brychta

OXFORD

UNIVERSITY PRESS

A man came to Kipper's class. He was called Mr Molar. He made everyone laugh.

Mr Molar had a puppet. "This is Freddie Floss," he said.

"Hello, children," said the puppet in a funny voice.

"Oh dear!" said Mr Molar. "Look at Freddie's teeth."

"Ugh!" said everyone. "They're horrible."

The puppet had black spots on his
teeth. One tooth was missing.

"He hasn't been cleaning them
properly," said Mr Molar.

"You must always clean your teeth
properly," said Mr Molar.

"If you do, they will look like this!" he said. The puppet's teeth were now shiny and white.

Kipper was playing with his yo-yo, and telling Mum about Mr Molar. He spun the yo-yo round very fast. Oh no! It hit him in the mouth.

He began to cry. "Is my tooth broken?" he asked. "It really, really hurts."

"I don't think it's broken," said
Mum, "but we should let the dentist
look at it, just in case."

Kipper was worried. "Is it going to hurt?" he asked.

"Of course not," said Mum. "You'll like the dentist. He's good fun."

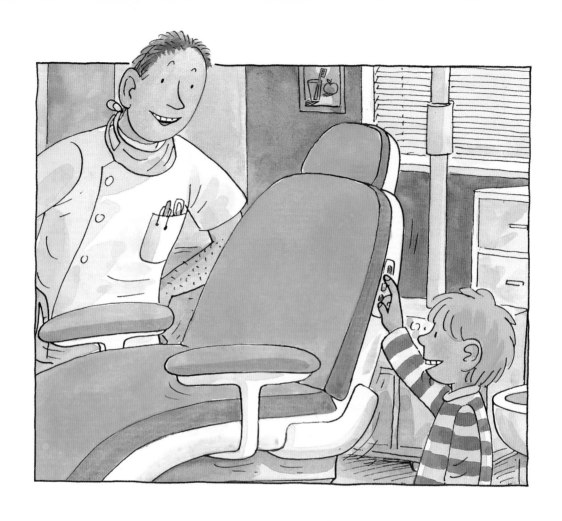

"This is my flying chair," said the dentist. He let Kipper press the button and the chair went up and down.

"Lie back in the flying chair," he said. "I'll just put this bright light on and look at your teeth."

"Your front tooth is fine," said the
dentist. "But there's a little black
spot on this back tooth."

"First I'm going to clean the spot.
Then I'll dry it and put a filling in
it," he said.

"What is a black spot?" asked
Kipper.

"It means the tooth is just starting
to go bad," said the dentist.

"You can get holes in your teeth," he said, "if you don't clean them every day, and if you eat lots of sweets."

The dentist gave Kipper a tablet
to chew. Soon, there were little
specks of red on his teeth.

"My tongue is red, too," said
Kipper.

"The specks show where you haven't cleaned your teeth and gums very well," said the dentist. He showed Kipper how to brush his teeth properly.

Mum bought some tablets and some new toothbrushes.

"I'm going to clean my teeth properly from now on," said Kipper.

Kipper told Dad, Biff and Chip
about the dentist. "I've got
something for you," he said. He
gave them each a tablet to chew.

Biff and Chip chewed the tablets,
but they had only a few red specks
on their teeth.

"We clean them well," said Chip.

Dad began to go out of the room.

"Come back, Dad," called Kipper.

"Show us your teeth."

"Hmmm!" said Dad.

"Oh Dad!" said Kipper. "Look at your red teeth! I'll show you how to clean them properly."

Talk about the story

Why did the children say 'ugh!' when they saw Freddie Floss's teeth?

How did Kipper feel when he hurt his tooth?

Why did the dentist give Kipper a tablet to chew?

Have you ever hurt yourself? Who helped to make it better?

How to clean your teeth

Start with the outsides of your teeth – first on the top, then on the bottom.

Put the brush like this, against your teeth and gums.

Use small circular movements. Don't scrub!

Then do the insides – first on the top, then on the bottom.

You can hold the toothbrush like this when you do the insides.

Then clean the tops of your molars (the chewing surfaces). Here it is OK to scrub.

And then, to feel if they are clean, run your tongue over all your teeth. Rinse out and you're done!

Find the twins

Find the two pictures of Freddie that are exactly the same.

First Experiences

At the Vet — Roderick Hunt • Alex Brychta — F·I·R·S·T E·X·P·E·R·I·E·N·C·E·S
At the Dentist — Roderick Hunt • Alex Brychta — F·I·R·S·T E·X·P·E·R·I·E·N·C·E·S
At School — Roderick Hunt • Alex Brychta — F·I·R·S·T E·X·P·E·R·I·E·N·C·E·S
At the Pool — Roderick Hunt • Alex Brychta — F·I·R·S·T E·X·P·E·R·I·E·N·C·E·S

Books for children to read and enjoy

The Snowman — Cynthia Rider • Alex Brychta
Super Dad — Roderick Hunt • Alex Brychta
Dragon Danger — Cynthia Rider • Alex Brychta
Arctic Adventure — Roderick Hunt • Alex Brychta
The Hairy-Scary Monster — Cynthia Rider • Alex Brychta

Level 1: Getting Ready
Level 2: Starting to Read
Level 3: Becoming a Reader
Level 4: Building Confidence
Level 5: Reading with Confidence

OXFORD
UNIVERSITY PRESS

Great Clarendon Street,
Oxford OX2 6DP

Text © Roderick Hunt and
Annemarie Young 2007
Illustrations © Alex Brychta 2007

First published 2007

Series Editors: Kate Ruttle, Annemarie Young

British Library Cataloguing in Publication Data available

ISBN: 978-019-838656-8

10 9 8 7 6 5 4 3 2 1

Printed in China by Imago

With thanks to
Tony Holland BDS,
LDS RCS

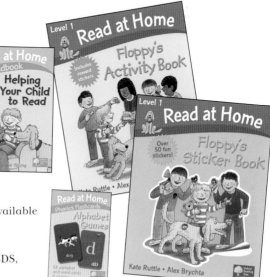